Photo by Danna Segrest

A scene from The Purple Rose Theatre Company production of *Months on End*.

MONTHS ON END
BY CRAIG POSPISIL

DRAMATISTS
PLAY SERVICE
INC.

MONTHS ON END
Copyright © 2003, Craig Allan Pospisil

All Rights Reserved

CAUTION: Professionals and amateurs are hereby warned that performance of MONTHS ON END is subject to payment of a royalty. It is fully protected under the copyright laws of the United States of America, and of all countries covered by the International Copyright Union (including the Dominion of Canada and the rest of the British Commonwealth), and of all countries covered by the Pan-American Copyright Convention, the Universal Copyright Convention, the Berne Convention, and of all countries with which the United States has reciprocal copyright relations. All rights, including professional/amateur stage rights, motion picture, recitation, lecturing, public reading, radio broadcasting, television, video or sound recording, all other forms of mechanical or electronic reproduction, such as CD-ROM, CD-I, DVD, information storage and retrieval systems and photocopying, and the rights of translation into foreign languages, are strictly reserved. Particular emphasis is placed upon the matter of readings, permission for which must be secured from the Author's agent in writing.

The English language stock and amateur stage performance rights in the United States, its territories, possessions and Canada for MONTHS ON END are controlled exclusively by DRAMATISTS PLAY SERVICE, INC., 440 Park Avenue South, New York, NY 10016. No professional or nonprofessional performance of the Play may be given without obtaining in advance the written permission of DRAMATISTS PLAY SERVICE, INC., and paying the requisite fee.

Inquiries concerning all other rights should be addressed to Beacon Artists Agency, 208 West 30th Street, Suite 401, New York, NY 10001. Attn: Patricia McLaughlin.

SPECIAL NOTE
Anyone receiving permission to produce MONTHS ON END is required to give credit to the Author as sole and exclusive Author of the Play on the title page of all programs distributed in connection with performances of the Play and in all instances in which the title of the Play appears for purposes of advertising, publicizing or otherwise exploiting the Play and/or a production thereof. The name of the Author must appear on a separate line, in which no other name appears, immediately beneath the title and in size of type equal to 50% of the size of the largest, most prominent letter used for the title of the Play. No person, firm or entity may receive credit larger or more prominent than that accorded the Author. The following acknowledgment must appear on the title page in all programs distributed in connection with performances of the Play:

Originally produced by The Purple Rose Theatre Company.
Jeff Daniels — Executive Director
Guy Sanville — Artistic Director
Alan Ribant — Managing Director

For my friends,

*Wade Richards,
John Powell
&
Jay Zimmerman*

ACKNOWLEDGMENTS

The development of *Months on End* has been an interesting journey. It started life as a very different kind of play but evolved into the script published here. There are a number of people who helped and encouraged me as *Months on End* evolved, and I'd like to thank them for their time, creativity and support. They are, in roughly chronological order:

Diana Wells (for a keen editorial eye); Jay Zimmerman, John Livingstone and Lona McManus (for sending me in a different direction); Judy Boals; Eleanore Speert; the members of the Workshop at the Neighborhood Playhouse — especially Harold Baldridge, Jim Brill (theatrical facilitator extraordinaire), Steven Ditmyer & Darcie Siciliano (who will always be Heidi to me); Cal Skaags (who I can't thank enough); the family of Wade Richards; Stephen Sultan; Patricia Watt & the Manhattan Drama Collective; Jamie Richards & the Ensemble Studio Theatre; Robert Lewis Vaughan; Patricia McLaughlin; Deborah Hedwall; Emma Walton, Sybil Christopher & the Bay Street Theatre; everyone at the Purple Rose Theatre Company — especially Suzi Regan, Sandy Birch, Ryan Carlson & Guy Sanville; and, finally, Brooke Fulton (for being with me in Michigan and more).

Craig Pospisil
November 2002
New York

MONTHS ON END was originally produced by The Purple Rose Theatre Company (Jeff Daniels, Executive Director; Guy Sanville, Artistic Director; Alan Ribant, Managing Director) in Chelsea, Michigan, on January 25, 2002. It was directed by Suzi Regan; the set design was by Andew Gorney; the lighting design was by Rob Murphy; the sound design was by Suzi Regan; the prop design was by Danna Segrest; the costume design was by Colleen Ryan-Peters; and the stage manager was Amy Hickman. The cast was as follows:

WALTER	Wayne David Parker
ELAINE	Sandra Birch
PHOEBE	Martie Sanders
BEN	Edward M. Nahhat
TONY	Trevor Rosen
NICK	Ryan Carlson
PAIGE	Michelle Held
HEIDI	Inga R. Wilson
GWEN	Trudy Mason
CHRIS	Will David Young

AUTHOR'S NOTE

Despite the multiple locations in this play, I want to stress that I don't intend, expect or even want fully realized sets for each scene. The sets for the scenes should be minimal; suggested rather than realistic. Use the bare minimum needed to convey the sense of place, and be cautious about adding things.

I suggest you divide your stage into four or five playing spaces with the set pieces for each in place at the beginning of the play or act break. This means the lights can go down on one scene and rise almost immediately on the next. And many of the scenes have common elements that would allow for sets/playing spaces to be doubled or reused. What you should avoid is long or involved set changes between the scenes. Everyone hates seeing stagehands dressed in black come out and rearrange the furniture, and it would slow the pace of the show too much, easily adding ten to fifteen minutes to your running time.

If you do want to have some kind of change, then choreograph some kind of transitions between scenes, something that will keep the flow of the play moving. Be creative and make it part of the show as a whole.

Finally, I think the play may be short enough to be performed straight through without a break, but if you want to have an intermission it should come after the "June" scene.

CHARACTERS

WALTER — in his 30s

ELAINE — in her early 30s

PHOEBE — a friend of Elaine's, 33

BEN — Phoebe's fiancé, 30s

TONY — friend of Nick's, 20s/30s

NICK — Walter's brother, also 30s

PAIGE — Nick's girlfriend, late 20s/early 30s

HEIDI — Phoebe's younger sister, 22

GWEN — Phoebe's mother 50s/60s

CHRIS —Phoebe's father, 50s/60s

PLACE

Various locations in and near New York City; a beach in Mexico; a hotel room in Los Angeles.

TIME

The present.

SCENE BREAKDOWN

JANUARY — Walter, Elaine
FEBRUARY — Ben, Phoebe, Tony
MARCH — Paige, Nick
APRIL — Phoebe, Elaine, Ben
MAY — Heidi
JUNE — Phoebe, Elaine, Gwen, Chris, Heidi
JULY — Walter, Nick, Tony
AUGUST — Phoebe, Ben, Heidi, Elaine, Paige
SEPTEMBER — Gwen, Chris, Phoebe
OCTOBER — Ben, Walter
NOVEMBER — Ben, Phoebe
DECEMBER — Walter, Nick

MONTHS ON END

JANUARY

The stage is in darkness.

PARTY VOICES. … three … two … one … Happy New Year! *(There are cheers, the sounds of noisemakers and champagne corks popping. The strains of "Auld Lang Syne" are perhaps also heard. The lights come up on Elaine, a depressed-looking woman in her early thirties. She wears an evening dress and nurses a glass of champagne. She has already had several. She surveys the party with distaste. Walter, also in his thirties, enters. He wears a tuxedo. He notices Elaine by herself and crosses to her.)*
WALTER. Well … a new year.
ELAINE. Yeah.
WALTER. So far it feels pretty much like last year.
ELAINE. Which sucked.
WALTER. Well, it's less than a minute old. Give it time.
ELAINE. To really, really suck.
WALTER. *(Pause.)* Last year was bad for you then?
ELAINE. The. Worst.
WALTER. Why? Or shouldn't I ask?
ELAINE. Well, let's see … it began with my dog dying of kidney failure.
WALTER. Oh, I'm sorry. That's a hard thing.
ELAINE. I'd just moved. Been in my new place for about a week when all of a sudden she stops eating. Stops moving really.
WALTER. How old was she?
ELAINE. Fifteen.

WALTER. That's pretty old for a dog, isn't it?
ELAINE. Oh, she was old so she deserved to die?
WALTER. No, course not. I just mean they don't live much longer than that normally. I'm sure she had a good life.
ELAINE. I guess. I just miss her little face when I come home at night. She always perked me up.
WALTER. That's the nice thing about a pet. That unconditional love.
ELAINE. There certainly wasn't any other face to greet me when I got home.
WALTER. Ah, yes. Being alone can be hard ... but I think solitude is underrated. It's important to have time by yourself. To just ... be. *(Slight pause.)* Relationships can be harder than being alone sometimes.
ELAINE. Tell me about it. I've spent plenty of time in relationship hell.
WALTER. That's not quite what I meant, but ... well, it's hard to find the right person.
ELAINE. No, I find all too many of them. I've had nine boyfriends in the last year.
WALTER. And they say all the good men are married or gay.
ELAINE. Although, calling them boyfriends is a stretch. The only reason I can do it is because I changed my definition. *(Slight pause.)* I mean, just when does a guy change from a date into a boyfriend? Is it walks in the park? Holding hands at the movies? Who knows. *(Slight pause.)* So, I decided that a guy becomes a boyfriend after four dates or the first time he stays for breakfast. Whichever comes first. *(Slight pause.)* And bang ... within a couple of months I was able to say I'd had three boyfriends.
WALTER. Congratulations. I guess.
ELAINE. Yeah, now I don't feel like I'm alone, just a loser. *(Slight pause.)* They all dumped me, of course. A little after the fifth date I started hearing, "I'm not ready for a big commitment," or "I need to find out who I am first," or "I've got to get home to my wife."
WALTER. At least they came out and said, "That's it." Not everyone does that. Some people go for years wanting to get out of a relationship, but they're too scared to say anything. Or they don't know how. *(Slight pause.)* Consider yourself lucky.

ELAINE. You're driving me nuts, you know that.
WALTER. Am I? I'm sorry.
ELAINE. Stop trying to put a positive spin on everything. It's New Year's Eve. People are supposed to be depressed. *(Slight pause.)* The whole holiday is made up anyway.
WALTER. Aren't they all?
ELAINE. Oh, shut up.
WALTER. Look, things could always be worse. Don't go around adding up everything that's wrong with your life. You've got to focus on what's right.
ELAINE. Is that supposed to make me feel better?
WALTER. A little, yes.
ELAINE. Well, it doesn't! *(Slight pause.)* I hate that philosophy. Sure, things could be worse. I could have cancer. There could be a nuclear war. The Earth could decide to stop spinning on its axis. *(Slight pause.)* So what?! Does that make me any less lonely? Will I sleep better tonight? *(She puts the glass down and digs in her purse for a Kleenex. She blows her nose loudly and starts to cry.)* Christ, how did I wind up here? Every damn New Year's I find myself at some stranger's apartment. And they're always living better lives than me. Look at this place. It's enormous.
WALTER. Oh, don't fall into that trap. Just because someone has money doesn't mean they're happy.
ELAINE. You really have to stop that. *(Slight pause.)* What makes it worse, too, is these people have no taste. Did you see that painting in the other room? What is that? It looks like a leprechaun on acid.
WALTER. So, what brought you here?
ELAINE. *What* indeed. *(Slight pause.)* I'm on a date. A really, really lousy date.
WALTER. Oh? Where is he?
ELAINE. See that guy over there by the kitchen door? The one with the curly, dark hair? The one with the broad shoulders and great cheekbones?
WALTER. The one kissing my wife?
ELAINE. Yeah. *(She does a double take.)* What?
WALTER. You weren't the only one having a bad year.
ELAINE. But you … how can…? Oh, God, I'm sorry.
WALTER. Why? You're not kissing her.

ELAINE. Yeah, but here I am going on and on about ... I mean, this is only our third date and no breakfast. That's your wife.
WALTER. It seems like I've been waiting for this moment for months. The element of surprise is gone.
ELAINE. Still, I mean ... hey ... where'd they go?
WALTER. Down the hall to the bedroom.
ELAINE. How can you just stand there? Why don't you leave?
WALTER. I live here. With the leprechaun.
ELAINE. My, this year is off to a good start. *(Pause.)* I'm sorry.
WALTER. No, forget it. I hate it too. Nina did most of the decorating. The only thing I like are the African masks.
ELAINE. Oh, yes, yes. Those are lovely. *(Pause.)* I think maybe I'll go. Except my coat's in the bedroom.
WALTER. Would you like a glass of champagne?
ELAINE. I think I've had enough.
WALTER. Are you sure? It's very good champagne.
ELAINE. Yes, I know. It's quickly replacing all the blood in my brain.
WALTER. Well, if you won't drink any, would you at least help me pour it down the drain?
ELAINE. Pour Dom Perignon down the drain? Why?
WALTER. It occurs to me that if the champagne was gone maybe all these people would decide to leave. And head to the bedroom for their coats.
ELAINE. *(Slight pause.)* Why, yes, I could use another glass.
WALTER. Right this way. *(Slight pause.)* Oh, wait ... what's your name?
ELAINE. Elaine.
WALTER. I'm Walter.
ELAINE. Nice to meet you.
WALTER. You too. Here's to a New Year. *(Walter offers Elaine his arm and they exit. Fade to black.)*

FEBRUARY

Phoebe and Ben, in their early thirties, sit at a small café table drinking coffee. Phoebe has a bright red scarf looped around her neck and two or three bride's magazines open in front of her.

PHOEBE. What about this one?
BEN. Yeah, that's gorgeous too.
PHOEBE. Do you like it better than these?
BEN. I … I don't know. They're all very pretty. *(Ben looks at his watch.)*
PHOEBE. Ben, can you stop checking your watch?
BEN. Phoebe, I don't have time for this right now. I've got to have the plans for that apartment renovation ready to show the client first thing tomorrow, so I'll be lucky if I'm home by eleven. And my CD player's broken so I can't even listen to the Beatles while I work.
PHOEBE. Hey, I'm meeting Elaine and my mother and sister in an hour to go wedding dress shopping. I need your help.
BEN. And you've got it. But you know you're going to have to try them on and see what looks best. *(Slight pause.)* Isn't this bad luck, anyway? Aren't I *not* supposed to see your dress before the wedding?
PHOEBE. No, you're just not supposed to see me *in* it. *(Slight pause.)* I think. *(Slight pause.)* Oh, who knows. The whole "not seeing the bride" thing is probably void once you've lived together for five years. We're probably doomed already.
BEN. Oh that's a great attitude.
PHOEBE. No, I'm serious. We are.
BEN. Phoebe …
PHOEBE. No, no. We're doomed, and you have to go back to work, so go. Screw the dress. I won't wear one.
BEN. Don't be like this.
PHOEBE. Like what? What am I being like?

BEN. Nothing, just ... Show me the dresses again.
PHOEBE. No, no, no. You go back to the office. Draw your blueprints or whatever. I'll do everything. I'll find the hall, pick the invitations, the flowers. Don't worry, I'll let you know when and where you need to show up for the wedding well in advance.
BEN. That's not fair. We've talked about those things — flowers, patterns, music — but you never like my ideas.
PHOEBE. I'm not walking down the aisle to "I Want to Hold Your Hand."
BEN. That was a joke.
PHOEBE. This whole damn thing is a joke. I don't even know why we're getting married.
BEN. How am I supposed to respond to that?
PHOEBE. Well, you could at least try.
BEN. I am trying. I've been trying. And if you showed me three or four dresses you liked, or asked, you know, like, veil or no veil, I could have an opinion. But you've got a couple dozen here. I don't know. What do you want?
PHOEBE. I don't know.
BEN. Why not?
PHOEBE. Because I never get what I want.
BEN. What's that supposed to mean?
PHOEBE. Nothing. Forget it.
BEN. No. What? You can't say something like that ...
PHOEBE. *(Overlapping.)* Nothing, okay? Nothing. Listen, uh ... Wade called.
BEN. What? Why?
PHOEBE. He passed out while leading a tour at the museum.
BEN. Oh my God. Is he okay?
PHOEBE. Yeah, but he spent a couple days in the hospital, and now he's afraid to travel alone. He asked if his sister could come to the wedding with him. So Paige's coming too, all right?
BEN. Yeah, of course. Of course.
PHOEBE. *(Pause.)* Are you okay?
BEN. Wade pushes himself too hard.
PHOEBE. I know.
BEN. Damn it. I mean, he should ... In high school we'd say that we'd be like uncles to each other's kids.

PHOEBE. I know.
BEN. And I'm going to hold him to that.
PHOEBE. Sounds good to me.
BEN. *(Pause.)* I like that dress.
PHOEBE. The slinky one. That's my favorite too.
BEN. See? I knew you didn't need me. I'll see you at home. *(Ben kisses Phoebe and exits the café. Phoebe watches him go a little sadly. She looks down at her bridal magazines and flips them shut with a sigh. Tony, in his late twenties or early thirties, enters, shaking off his jacket and shivering from the cold outside. He looks around the space and sees Phoebe. He smiles and hurries over. Phoebe looks up, startled, when Tony sits down. He starts speaking before she has a chance to say anything.)*
TONY. Jenna, hi! I'm Tony. Sorry I'm late. All the snow slowed me down. Listen, I hope you don't have plans tonight, 'cause I had this wild impulse on the way over here and I stopped at Lincoln Center and got two tickets to the ballet. I thought we could go for a drink first, then to the ballet, and then I made reservations for a late dinner at the Supper Club. They're gonna have a swing band, and I thought we could have some great food and take a few passes on the dance floor. *(Slight pause.)* Whadya say?
PHOEBE. Well, ah … that sounds great … but …
TONY. What?
PHOEBE. I'm not Jenna.
TONY. *(Slight pause.)* But you're wearing a red scarf.
PHOEBE. Well, it's cold out. And I'm still not Jenna.
TONY. *(Slight pause.)* Right, okay, well, thanks. Sorry I bothered you. God, what an idiot.
PHOEBE. Oh, no. I thought it was lovely.
TONY. Really?
PHOEBE. Yeah.
TONY. Oh, that's great. You don't know how long I spent trying to think of something that would really grab you. I mean, her. *(Slight pause.)* You think it'll work?
PHOEBE. Yeah, sure. I'd go out with you.
TONY. Really? Cool! I was kinda worried 'cause this is, like, a blind date, through the personals.
PHOEBE. Yeah, I guessed.
TONY. Well, hey … thanks for listening. *(Tony stands and looks*

around the room. He doesn't see another red scarf anywhere. Phoebe watches him.)
PHOEBE. How late are you?
TONY. Not much. Ten, fifteen minutes.
PHOEBE. Oh, that's not bad.
TONY. Maybe twenty.
PHOEBE. Still. *(Slight pause.)* Can you call her?
TONY. Oh! Duh! Yeah, I've got her cell phone number. *(Tony pulls out a cellular telephone and dials. He listens for a moment and then disconnects.)* Wrong number. *(He rummages in his wallet, pulls out a scrap of paper and checks it against the number on his cell phone.)*
PHOEBE. Dialed wrong?
TONY. … no, this is the number she gave me.
PHOEBE. Oh. Well, maybe you wrote it down wrong. You know, flipped a couple of numbers.
TONY. You know … I don't think so. Anyway, sorry I bothered you.
PHOEBE. Oh, no, hey, I'm sure you just mixed up the numbers. Or she did. Hell, I screw up my own number all the time.
TONY. Well, thanks, but I think I've been had. And I don't even like the ballet.
PHOEBE. Oh, wait … give her the benefit of the doubt. *(Slight pause.)* Or you know, if she did give you the wrong number, then she's not worth your time.
TONY. Yeah. I guess.
PHOEBE. And give the ballet another chance too. If you see the right one, it can really be beautiful.
TONY. Okay. Hey, thanks. You've been great. And you don't even know me. That's cool.
PHOEBE. It was fun.
TONY. Hey … what's your name?
PHOEBE. *(Slight pause.)* Phoebe.
TONY. Listen, ah … I mean, would you — *(Tony's cell phone rings.)*
TONY. Hello? Oh … Jenna. *(Slight pause.)* Ah, no, no, that's fine. I was late too. *(Slight pause.)* Yeah, I can wait. Sure. See you soon. *(He hangs up, looks at Phoebe. Pause.)* The snow slowed her down too.
PHOEBE. Yeah, it does that. *(Slight pause.)* Here, the place is full. Why don't you take this table.
TONY. Oh, no, you stay. I'll find one.

PHOEBE. No, really. I've got to go anyway. *(Phoebe gathers her stuff.)*
TONY. Well, okay. Thanks again.
PHOEBE. Sure. Good luck. *(Phoebe exits as Tony takes a seat at the table. He watches her leave. Blackout.)*

MARCH

A beach in Mexico about an hour after sunset. Nick, in his thirties, is on all fours, searching the ground intently. Paige, late twenties, enters. She carries a flashlight and a sieve. She stops a few feet from Nick and watches him for a moment as he continues to search.

PAIGE. Any luck?
NICK. Oh, sure. I found the ring an hour ago. I'm down here looking through the sand for gold doubloons now.
PAIGE. Look, Nick, I'm sorry.
NICK. I heard you the first fifty times.
PAIGE. I thought these might help. I borrowed a flashlight from the front desk and a sieve from the kitchen.
NICK. A sieve?
PAIGE. Yeah, I thought you could scoop up sand and sift through it. The ring won't go through the holes.
NICK. Oh. *(Pause.)* Thanks. *(Nick takes the sieve from her and starts to use it. Paige stands by awkwardly, unsure of whether to stay or go.)*
PAIGE. I'm sorry.
NICK. Paige …
PAIGE. But I want to help.
NICK. Look … thanks for the sieve. It's a good idea. But I'd rather do this alone.
PAIGE. *(Slight pause.)* It's just I had no idea.
NICK. Really.
PAIGE. It was very romantic, though. Very sweet.

NICK. Which explains your reaction. *(Long pause.)*
PAIGE. Listen, Nicky …
NICK. If you're gonna stand there would you at least shine the flashlight over here?
PAIGE. Oh, sure. *(She turns on the flashlight and shines it across the ground in front of Nick.)*
NICK. Thanks.
PAIGE. Listen, I talked to the hotel manager … there aren't any other rooms available.
NICK. Terrific.
PAIGE. Well, it's high season. They're booked up. *(Pause.)* I'm sorry.
NICK. Doesn't matter. You take it. *(They do not speak for a while as Nick sifts through the sand.)*
PAIGE. Nick, this is pointless. You don't even know if you're looking in the right place. It might've flown five feet to the right or left. It's lost. Look, I'll pay for the ring.
NICK. It's not the money.
PAIGE. Then what is it?
NICK. It was my grandmother's wedding ring.
PAIGE. Oh.
NICK. If I don't find it my father will … well, he probably won't do anything. He'll just look sad and nod his head, and say, "Well … I guess you can't keep something forever." And I can't take it when he does that
PAIGE. Here, lemme give you a hand. *(Paige kneels down and begins feeling across the sand. Nick grabs her arm.)*
NICK. I don't need your help, okay?
PAIGE. But, Nick, you could look all night and never find it.
NICK. Would you go away please?!
PAIGE. But I want to do something. I feel like this is all my fault.
NICK. It is!
PAIGE. Hey! I'm bending over backwards trying to apologize here! I feel bad enough. You're supposed to say something like, "Oh, it's not your fault."
NICK. But it is.
PAIGE. It's just as much your fault.
NICK. Me?! All I did was ask you to marry me. You're the one who answered by throwing the ring away!

PAIGE. I did not! I flinched. And you didn't even ask.
NICK. What?!
PAIGE. You couldn't even say the words.
NICK. You didn't let me finish!
PAIGE. So you admit you didn't ask me.
NICK. You cut me off! I held out the ring and all I got a chance to say was, "Paige, will you —" ... and then you screamed and knocked it away.
PAIGE. No, no, no. You suddenly stopped and mumbled something about a present. And then you pulled out this ring and grabbed my left hand.
NICK. And you knocked it away!
PAIGE. I flinched! It was an automatic reaction to being surprised.
NICK. You screamed.
PAIGE. I was *very* surprised!
NICK. You know, I don't feel like debating this whole thing. I've gotta find this ring. If you wanna help ... fine, but I'm not talking about it. *(He searches the sand again.)*
PAIGE. I'm sorry I can't marry you.
NICK. Oh, Christ.
PAIGE. No, really. I am. I just have to tell you, it's nothing you did, but ... I was going to breakup with you when we got home. I thought the trip would be like ... ending on a high note. *(Slight pause.)* Isn't that weird?
NICK. I'll try to savor the irony later. *(Pause.)* End on a high note? Why do you tell me this? What, it's not enough you don't want to marry me?
PAIGE. No, look, I didn't want to hurt you. I wanted to give you something before I ended it. I thought I should tell you.
NICK. You know that's twisted, right? That's like giving your child some candy before you spank them.
PAIGE. Okay, so fine. Maybe it wasn't my best idea, but you and me ... it just isn't working.
NICK. Where do you get that? This is, like, the first real fight we've had. To me that sounds like things are working pretty well.
PAIGE. Not fighting isn't the same as being happy. We're different people. We look at things from different angles. *(Slight pause.)* Like this trip. You wanted to come here to lie on a beach and I

wanted to go see the Mayan ruins.
NICK. Right, so we decided to do both.
PAIGE. But after a day on a beach I'm bored stiff. And the only thing about the Mayan cities that got your attention was that they sacrificed virgins. See? Same place, but totally different vacations in mind.
NICK. I think that's bullshit. It says we're able to compromise. Did I want to climb some old building? No. But I was gonna do it because you wanted to. You want to see it differently ... well, I guess that makes your point for you. But I still disagree.
PAIGE. *(Slight pause.)* Why did you ask me?
NICK. The regular reasons, I guess. I thought you were The One.
PAIGE. The One?!? You thought I was "The One"?! Are you nuts?
NICK. Well, I guess so.
PAIGE. The One? There's no such thing! Why don't you just call me the Easter Bunny?! I can't believe you'd say that!
NICK. Hey, I'm the one who bared my heart and soul and all that crap. You're the one who said "no."
PAIGE. You're damn right.
NICK. I paid you a fucking compliment! What are you upset about?!
PAIGE. The One. I mean, what does that mean? It's all fate and destiny and predetermined ... shit. It's such a stupid idea that there's only one person out there for each of us.
NICK. Hey, I'll get over you, if that's what you're worried about.
PAIGE. Good.
NICK. There's hundreds of others just like you all over New York.
PAIGE. Damn straight!
NICK. Hell, there's women as good as you in that bar down the beach. Maybe I'll go pick one of them up and take her back to our room.
PAIGE. That's the spirit.
NICK. I don't know what the hell we're talking about!
PAIGE. There are billions of people on this dumb planet. Talk about a needle in a haystack. The One. I mean, the odds are we don't even speak the same language. Or he's gay.
NICK. How could a guy be The One if he's gay. Wouldn't that kinda disqualify him?

PAIGE. No. Life is that cruel. Very short and very cruel.
NICK. *(Pause.)* Are we talking about you or your brother?
PAIGE. I'm not *not* marrying you because Wade is sick.
NICK. But…?
PAIGE. … but I guess it means you strip away the stuff that isn't essential. Wade says he doesn't have time to deal with something … or someone that isn't absolutely necessary. And I think maybe that should always be the case. I love you, Nicky, but I know I'm not *in* love with you. *(Long pause.).* I'm sorry about the ring.
NICK. Well … I guess you can't keep something forever. *(Pause.)* You know, I think I'll get a drink. One of the things I wanted to do most here was lie on the beach under the stars with you drinking margaritas. What do you say?
PAIGE. I don't think so. If I started drinking I'd start crying. *(Slight pause.)* I'm sorry. I keep turning you down tonight.
NICK. That's okay. *(They sit on the beach close to one another, looking out. Fade to black.)*

APRIL

> *A living room. Phoebe and Elaine sit on a couch. They each have a glass of wine. Phoebe removes a new video camera, a present, from its box and plays with it as they talk.*

BEN. *(Offstage.)* Phoebe, don't we have any curry?
PHOEBE. Not unless it's in the spice rack. Ben, are you sure you don't need a hand in there?
BEN. *(Offstage.)* No. Everything'll be ready soon.
ELAINE. What's he cooking?
PHOEBE. He won't tell me. *(There is a crash heard from the kitchen.)* It's a surprise.
BEN. *(Offstage.)* Don't come in. Everything's fine.
ELAINE. Oh, you're so lucky.
PHOEBE. Lucky we'll be getting new dishes soon, it sounds like.

ELAINE. Phoebe, I'd kill for someone who'd cook me dinner.
PHOEBE. Yeah, and it's very sweet, but I wanted to go out. I wanted to go to that new French-Asian fusion restaurant that just opened downtown.
ELAINE. Oh, I read about that one. No, you can never talk in those trendy places. There's too many people. It's too noisy.
PHOEBE. That's just what Ben said. I swear you two are like peas in a pod. Maybe the two of you should get married.
ELAINE. Don't think I wouldn't, if he weren't so hung up on you.
PHOEBE. What's wrong with going to a place that might be a bit loud or exciting? Ben always wants to go to these little, candlelit restaurants.
ELAINE. That's romantic.
PHOEBE. Yeah, they're romantic, but that's the only sort of place he wants to go. I like to go to lots of different places. It just starts to wear at me.
ELAINE. Do you tell him that?
PHOEBE. Yes.
ELAINE. In a nice way?
PHOEBE. Sometimes. But nothing changes. That's the way he's always been and always will be. For the rest of my life. *(Slight pause.)* Oh, God, let's talk about something else.
ELAINE. All right, well ... Happy Birthday, Phoebe! *(Elaine pulls a small wrapped gift out of her bag.)*
PHOEBE. Aaarrgh! I don't want to have this birthday.
ELAINE. Thirty-three isn't old.
PHOEBE. No numbers, please.
ELAINE. Oh, just open your present. *(Elaine hands her the gift, and Phoebe tears through the paper. She pulls out a pair of earrings.)*
PHOEBE. Oh. These are lovely.
ELAINE. They're for you to wear at the wedding. I got them at the museum gift shop. They're based on a pair of earrings in a Renaissance painting of an Italian wedding scene.
PHOEBE. Mmm. They're great.
ELAINE. Do you really like them?
PHOEBE. Oh, yeah. Thanks.
ELAINE. You're welcome. Say, do you have your list for me yet?
PHOEBE. What list?

ELAINE. Of who you want at your bridal shower.
PHOEBE. Yeah, I wrote down some names. I'll give it to you later. So, aside from work, what's up with you?
ELAINE. Not much. I signed up for a yoga class. Now, when's Heidi done with school? I want to make sure she's back in town for the shower.
PHOEBE. I don't remember. It's in my date book. Do you know my parents are giving her a car for graduation?
ELAINE. Wow. That's nice.
PHOEBE. I'll say. They never gave me a car.
ELAINE. You didn't graduate.
PHOEBE. Hey, don't you start. My mother's having a field day. "At least one of my girls will have a degree."
ELAINE. She's still on your case about that?
PHOEBE. She never stopped.
ELAINE. But it's not like you flunked out. You landed that great job at CBS.
PHOEBE. Oh, sure, and for the three years before the ratings dropped and I got fired, she shut up. But ever since it's been, "See? I told you journalism was a risky career, Phoebe."
BEN. *(Offstage.)* OOWW!!
PHOEBE. Are you okay?
BEN. *(Offstage.)* No problem. Just a hot pan.
ELAINE. Are you sure we can't help.
BEN. *(Offstage.)* No, no. It'll just be a minute.
ELAINE. Well, if we've got a minute, why don't you grab your date book?
PHOEBE. Why?
ELAINE. So we can pick a day for your shower.
PHOEBE. No, not tonight.
ELAINE. But I've got to start making calls.
PHOEBE. Yeah, I know. We'll talk later in the week. There's still time. *(Slight pause.)* Now talk to me … are you still dating that married guy?
ELAINE. His name is Walter.
PHOEBE. Well, I might think of him as "Walter" if I ever met him. So, what's going on?
ELAINE. It's nice. We have fun together.

PHOEBE. *(Slight pause.)* That's it? That's the whole report?
ELAINE. There's really not much to tell.
PHOEBE. Oh, sure, it's your average, everyday, illicit affair.
ELAINE. Don't remind me.
PHOEBE. Come on, Lainey, when do I get to meet him?
ELAINE. I don't know. What's the point? I mean, it's kind of a dead end, right?
PHOEBE. Why?
ELAINE. Because he's married!
PHOEBE. He's getting divorced.
ELAINE. Which makes me the girl he dates for a few months before moving on to find the next wife.
PHOEBE. You don't know that.
ELAINE. Oh, come on. How many times does something like this work? There's too much stuff in the way. When I'm at his place I keep wondering things like, did she keep her lingerie in this drawer? *(Slight pause.)* And the other morning … I couldn't help it. I snooped. I found a picture of him and Nina. A wedding picture. And I almost threw up. It just feels wrong to be dating a married man.
PHOEBE. So, why do you keep seeing him?
ELAINE. Well, you know, I mean … we have fun together. We went to the opening of this art gallery last week and … and I think I love him.
PHOEBE. Oh, my God, really?
ELAINE. Yeah. It's been great. *(Slight pause.)* And it's been torture. He and his wife fight over things, which upsets him, though he tries to hide it. And I don't know what to do. I don't know if he wants to talk about things, and I'm not sure I want to know. *(Slight pause.)* I don't want to be his rebound girl, Phoebe. That would hurt too much.
PHOEBE. Have you told him that?
ELAINE. No, of course not. That would involve a serious conversation and the risk of pain. And that must be avoided at all costs.
PHOEBE. Oh, sure. And pain postponed is always more fun.
ELAINE. It's so hard, because I don't know how long I can wait to find out if this is really something, or if it's some short-term romance. And I'm getting older too. You're not the only one. But am I about to get married? Am I in a stable relationship? Am I even

dating someone who's really available? No. No. Oh, and no. *(Slight pause.)* Oh, I hate it!! *(Slight pause.)* But, oh, I think I love him.
PHOEBE. *(Slight pause.)* That sucks.
ELAINE. Yeah.
PHOEBE. The four of us should go out sometime.
ELAINE. Yeah, that'd be nice.
PHOEBE. *(Slight pause.)* I think you should hang in there.
ELAINE. Yeah?
PHOEBE. Yeah.
ELAINE. Is it okay for me to still be your bridesmaid even though I'm an adulterous slut?
PHOEBE. Well, we'll have to sew a scarlet "A" on your ass, but other than that I don't see why not. *(Pause.)* We are two seriously fucked-up chicks.
ELAINE. Seriously.
PHOEBE. Thanks for the earrings. They're perfect for the wedding.
ELAINE. You're welcome. Thanks for being such a good friend. *(They hug. Ben enters, empty-handed.)*
BEN. How'd you like to go out for dinner?
ELAINE. What happened?
BEN. Don't ask. *(Slight pause.)* I'm sorry, Phoebe. I had this great meal planned.
PHOEBE. Well, it can't all be ruined. What's left?
BEN. Salad.
ELAINE. Well, hey, I'm on a diet anyway. *(The three of them exit to the kitchen. Blackout.)*

MAY

"Pomp and Circumstance" plays as the lights come up, and Heidi, a nervous young woman wearing a black graduation robe, enters and crosses to a podium. She carries a small stack of three-by-five note cards, which she refers to as she speaks.

HEIDI. Welcome. Welcome friends and family, welcome to our teachers ... and welcome to our parents. *(Slight pause.)* The day has finally come. The day this graduating class has been working towards for so many years of hard study. And I think I speak for my entire generation when I say ... thank you. *(Slight pause.)* Thank you to our parents. The people who lit the way. Who loved us and nurtured us. And who now cheer us on as we set out to face the challenges of tomorrow. *(Pause.)*

This class stands before you today poised to — *(The cards in her hand suddenly fly into the air, scattering around the podium. Heidi freezes and then looks at the cards lying around her on the floor. She tries to continue from memory.)* ... ah, poised to take on those challenges. We greet them with open arms. *(Pause.)* We, ah ... stand ... no, um ... *(She glances down to the cards on the ground, turning her head around to try and read some of them.)* It's wonderful for me to be able to stand here like this ... and look out ... Hold on, I'm sorry. *(Heidi stoops down and collects the cards, pulling them together randomly. She stands and smiles nervously at the audience.)*

And in those faces I see hope, idealism and ... no, that's wrong. *(She flips to the next card.)* We have spent four years at this school, studying hard and playing hard. And all of it has been part of our education, because — *(She goes to the next card.)* If you scratch our collective surface ... damn it. I'm sorry. I guess I should have numbered them. *(Next card.)* Welcome. ... no, did that one. *(Next card.)* Because college isn't just about reading Shakespeare or understanding the Theory of Relativity. These four years have been part of our evolution from adolescence to — *(Next card.)* ... a feeling of great loneliness ... *(Pause.)*

I'm very sorry. Just give me another moment. *(Heidi quickly spreads the cards out on the podium and reorders them. She begins again.)* All right ... The day has finally come. The day this class has been working towards for so many years of hard study. And I think I speak for my entire generation when I say ... oh, what's the point? *(Pause.)*

I mean, it's ruined, right? *(Slight pause.)* This is all my parents' fault. I was fine until they came by my room this morning, and my dad says to me, "Make it good, Heidi. Make sure they remember you." *(Slight pause.)* How's this? *(Slight pause.)*

Not that the speech was much good to begin with. I know these things are supposed to have a theme, but ... I mean, it's all been said already, hasn't it? And I'm sorry, but today just doesn't feel that momentous or anything. I know it's the end of one thing and the start of something else, but so what? Everything's like that. *(Slight pause.)* I don't know why I'm up here. I didn't want to give this address. Hell, I didn't even want to come to this college! I liked Vassar! But my dad went here. "It's a great school, Heidi. When you graduate from a place like this you can get a job anywhere." *(Pause.)*

Which would be great, if I had the slightest idea what I wanted to do with my life. *(Slight pause.)* I think that's the symptom of my generation's disease. We're caught between optimism and nihilism. You raised us to believe in limitless possibility. Consequently we have no idea how to choose anything. *(Slight pause.)* Not that there seems to be much point. The country is, what ... trillions of dollars in debt? And who knows if there will be any social security left by the time I retire, so why think about the future? *(Pause.)*

There'll be peace, you said. And racial harmony, sexual equality. Diseases will vanish. *(Pause.)* Uh-huh. *(Slight pause.)* Yeah, this from the people who were gonna save the world, but then decided to make a bundle on Wall Street instead. Kind of an oxymoron, don't you think, Mom? *(Slight pause.)* Was it too hard? Or did you just get bored? *(Pause.)*

And you wonder why we get tattoos and pierce our belly buttons, or eyebrows, or whatever. We're pissed off because you lied to us. *(Slight pause.)* Well, mainly, we're angry, because you took all the good drugs, had all the good sex, and then made all the good money. *(Slight pause.)* The only thing you're leaving for us is the bill. *(Pause.)*

I should probably stop here. *(Heidi looks over the cards on the podium and chooses one.)* And so, in closing, this class would like to say a heartfelt … thank you … to our parents. Thank you for loving us and taking care of us. *(Pause.)* We look forward to returning the favor in thirty or forty years. *(She exits. Fade to black.)*

JUNE

A changing room before a wedding. Phoebe, in a wedding dress, examines herself in a mirror. There is a side table nearby with her bouquet on top. Phoebe holds a lipstick case, which she opens and begins to apply lipstick to her lips. Her hand shakes, however, and she smears lipstick across her cheek. She stops and rubs away the errant traces. There is a sharp knock on the door, and Phoebe's mother, Gwen, breezes in.

GWEN. Thank God this day is finally here. If I had to deal with that caterer much longer I'd make you elope. *(Slight pause.)* How are you feeling?
PHOEBE. Good. Excited. *(Pause.)* Nervous as hell.
GWEN. Don't worry, Phoebe. Every bride feels that way. *(Slight pause.)* And no one could blame you for being nervous about marrying into that family. Ben's mother is a piece of work.
PHOEBE. Well, luckily I'm marrying Ben and not her, right?
GWEN. Oh, you marry the whole family, believe me. Your father's mother used to make these snide comments about me, but she always said them with a smile, so he never noticed. We'd get into such fights about his mother.
PHOEBE. Is my lipstick okay?
GWEN. Let's see. Oh, good Lord, no. *(Gwen licks her thumb and*

wipes at the offending smudges around Phoebe's mouth. Phoebe submits for a moment and then pulls away.)
PHOEBE. Mom ... Mom!
GWEN. You asked.
PHOEBE. I asked if it was okay. I didn't ask for a bath.
GWEN. Don't raise your voice at me. Between the caterer and that violinist you hired I don't need any more aggravation. She keeps stopping after each piece like she's finished playing. *(Slight pause.)* You look lovely.
PHOEBE. Thank you. And thanks for the dress. It means a lot to me that it was yours.
GWEN. That's so sweet. I'm just glad it fit.
PHOEBE. *(Slight pause.)* Thanks, Mom.
GWEN. What?
PHOEBE. We didn't have to let it out that much!
GWEN. Oh, now really. I didn't mean anything like that. I was very thin when I got married. Don't be so prickly.
PHOEBE. Do you even listen to yourself? As if I'm not nervous enough, you call me fat!
GWEN. I did not.
PHOEBE. "I was very thin when I got married." What the hell else is that supposed to mean?!
GWEN. Oh, you take everything as some kind of insult! Honestly, I don't know why you think I'm such an ogre. *(Heidi enters.)*
HEIDI. Ah, hello? Sound carries, you know. Everyone downstairs has barely noticed the violinist stopped playing.
GWEN. Didn't you check her references?
PHOEBE. Mom, why don't you go get her playing again.
GWEN. Fine. *(Slight pause.)* I love you.
PHOEBE. I love you too. *(They hug stiffly and Gwen hurries out. Heidi turns to Phoebe.)*
HEIDI. So, how's the blushing bride?
PHOEBE. Oh, I'm just peachy!
HEIDI. If it helps, Ben looks pretty nervous too.
PHOEBE. Yeah? Is Wade with him?
HEIDI. Yeah, he's trying to distract Ben with some old Monty Python routine, but Wade says it's a toss-up whether Ben says, "I do," or vomits on your shoes.

PHOEBE. He better not. I went into every store on Madison Avenue to find these.
HEIDI. Well, at least you didn't have to go through a big search for a dress, right?
PHOEBE. Oh, screw you, Heidi. It makes me look like a cow! How did I let Mom talk me into wearing this instead of that slinky Vera Wang I loved? What was I thinking?! A huge bow on my butt? Why didn't I just paint a big target there?
HEIDI. Hey, I think it looks good on you. It's got this great retro thing going for it.
PHOEBE. I didn't want a retro thing! *(Elaine bursts in, holding a blue garter.)*
ELAINE. Here! I got it!
PHOEBE. A garter?
ELAINE. Yeah. I bought it yesterday at a vintage clothing store, and I want it back, so it's old, new, borrowed and blue. Okay, stick your leg out.
PHOEBE. No.
HEIDI. You have to wear it.
PHOEBE. No, I don't.
HEIDI. You don't have anything blue.
PHOEBE. And I don't care. That whole thing is stupid.
ELAINE. Put it on.
PHOEBE. No.
HEIDI. Put it on! *(Heidi and Elaine grab Phoebe and wrestle her to the ground. Phoebe struggles and tries to get away, but finally submits and lets them put the garter on her leg.)*
PHOEBE. Okay, fine. But I'm not letting Ben take it off me in front of everyone. *(Elaine and Heidi look at each other.)*
ELAINE. Oh, great idea. I'll tell him.
PHOEBE. No, you won't! *(Elaine runs out, and Heidi stops Phoebe from going after her.)*
HEIDI. Whoa, whoa, listen ... I hate to tell you this, but you've only got a couple minutes to get ready.
PHOEBE. *(Pause.)* I need to fix my lipstick. Can you do it?
HEIDI. Ah ... I can try. I've never done it from this side. Oh, wait. Turn around and look in the mirror. *(Phoebe does, and Heidi stands behind her. She slides her arm around Phoebe and applies the*

lipstick looking over Phoebe's shoulder into the mirror.)
PHOEBE. Hey, not bad.
HEIDI. I guess this is what sisters are for.
PHOEBE. Would you marry Ben?
HEIDI. Excuse me?
PHOEBE. Would you?
HEIDI. Well, it doesn't matter if I would or not.
PHOEBE. So, you wouldn't?
HEIDI. No, I didn't say that. Look, what's the deal? Do you love him?
PHOEBE. Yes.
HEIDI. So, what's the problem?
PHOEBE. I'm freaking out! Does that mean inside I know this is wrong?
HEIDI. It means you're nervous. It's a big day, a big thing. *(Slight pause.)* Ben's terrific. He's got a great sense of humor. His taste in music is hopelessly stuck in the Sixties, but other than that, he's good for you. Everyone says so.
PHOEBE. That's 'cause you all get to sit back and watch. I'm the one who's doing this. *(There is a knock on the door and Phoebe's father, Chris, enters.)*
CHRIS. Hi, angel. Are you ready?
PHOEBE. No.
HEIDI. My cue to leave. *(To Chris.)* Make sure she comes down. *(Heidi sashays out.)*
CHRIS. What's wrong? *(Gwen reenters, holding a boutonniere.)*
GWEN. Chris, you forgot your boutonniere.
CHRIS. Oh, here, just give it to me.
GWEN. Oh, you'll never get it straight. Let me.
CHRIS. Then Phoebe will do it. You go ahead back down.
GWEN. What's going on? Everyone's waiting.
CHRIS. Nothing. Just give us a moment, will you please?
GWEN. Fine. I'm sure I don't want to know. *(Gwen exits, and Chris turns to Phoebe.)*
CHRIS. So what is it?
PHOEBE. I don't know if I can do this.
CHRIS. Well … you don't have to.
PHOEBE. What? DAD! You're supposed to tell me everything's

going to be all right. You're supposed to say, "Ben's great. You're perfect together." What're you doing to me?

CHRIS. There are no sure things. Your life with Ben will either work, or it won't.

PHOEBE. Oh, great! So what's the point?

CHRIS. Not taking risks doesn't mean you won't get hurt. *(Slight pause.)* Pretend you're in an airplane that's crashing —

PHOEBE. Why?

CHRIS. Just go with me on this. You're in a crashing plane, and you've got this parachute ... but it has some tears in it. If you stay in the plane ... ouch. But if you jump, maybe you'll be okay. Or maybe not, but it's your only chance.

PHOEBE. *(Slight pause.)* Are you calling Ben a torn parachute?

CHRIS. *(Pause.)* I don't think I've ever seen you make a big decision easily. When you were in grade school you used to sit at your desk and make lists of pros and cons when you had to make some big choice. I used to get such a kick out of that. I thought it was so considered and mature, but ... *(Slight pause.)* It's probably our fault. Maybe we made too many decisions for you, or didn't ... I don't know, didn't let life test you or something. It's hard, but sometimes it isn't about having more pros than cons. You know what you want. You don't need to wait until you can see it on paper.

PHOEBE. You're right. *(Chris holds the boutonniere out to Phoebe. She takes it and pins it to Chris' lapel. She kisses her father on the cheek and then wipes away the traces.)*

CHRIS. You're smudged. *(She quickly, expertly fixes her lipstick and picks up her bouquet.)*

PHOEBE. Okay ... where's that parachute? *(Smiling, Phoebe takes Chris' arm and they exit. Fade to black.)*

JULY

Walter, Nick and Tony are lounging on a beach. Nick and Tony stare out at the sand, surf and women. Walter reads a paperback book.

NICK. Tony, check her out!
TONY. Where?
NICK. The blonde over there. That is the reason bikinis were invented.
TONY. Oooo, she's hot. *(Walter looks over at the woman, but then goes back to his book.)*
NICK. Walt … Walt? Did you see her?
WALTER. Yeah, she's pretty.
NICK. Pretty? Hello? Pretty fantastic is more like it.
TONY. Definitely. She was stunning.
NICK. Almost gorgeous.
WALTER. I said she was pretty, what do you want?
NICK. I want you to get it right. Pretty? I mean, what is that? That's just a step above cute.
WALTER. All right, all right, she's very attractive.
NICK. Attractive?!
TONY. You're going backwards on us.
NICK. Tony was right the first time. Stunning.
TONY. Just a shade off gorgeous. Just a shade.
WALTER. Oh, really? Why? What's her fatal flaw?
NICK. She wasn't quite blonde enough. Nice hair, but not that really pure blonde.
TONY. There was some light brown in there.
WALTER. Oh, sure, yeah. That'll do it.
NICK. If just once …
WALTER. What do you want from me, Nick?
NICK. I want you to stop being such a drip. You're just sitting there reading. What's the matter with you?

WALTER. Is there some reason I can't sit and read? Did I miss the book-with-a-red-line-through-it sign as we came down down here?
NICK. You can read back at the house. I mean, would you go to a bar with us and bring a book?
WALTER. What's your deal? Just let me read. I'm not stopping you from lusting after these women.
NICK. Yeah, you are. You always do this.
TONY. Ah, let it go. It's okay.
NICK. No. It's not. *(To Walter.)* You are stopping me. 'Cause I know you're sitting there judging us. I can feel your disapproval, okay? You're worse than Mom. Screw you if you're so uptight. I like to look at women. If you wanna be all repressed, keep reading, but lose the attitude.
WALTER. Hey, I like to look at beautiful women too. I just don't like the way you talk about them. What're you, fourteen? Grow up.
NICK. Screw you *and* your political correctness. I'll talk about women any way I want. It's not like your sensitivity saved your marriage.
WALTER. *(A dangerous pause.)* Okay, that's it! *(Walter throws down his book and advances on Nick, who moves forward to meet him. They exchange shoves and it would escalate into a fight, but Tony separates them.)*
TONY. Hey guys, come on! The fireworks aren't until tonight. Plus we've got two more days out here. Save it for the train ride home at least.
NICK. *(Pause.)* All right, I'm sorry.
WALTER. Fine. *(Walter goes back to his book. Nick looks off down the beach. Tony is lost in thought. There is a silence. Tony leans over to Walter.)*
TONY. I … I don't get it. How else can you talk about women?
WALTER. All this … it's like watching porn. It's kind of fun at first, all the flesh and sex, but after ten minutes it gets really boring.
NICK. Boring?
WALTER. Yeah. It's just fucking. There's no feeling.
NICK. It's sexy!
WALTER. No, it's the exact opposite of sexy.
TONY. How's that?
WALTER. Well … what do you think is sexy?

TONY. Uh ... you know, a pretty girl, ah —
NICK. The babe in the bikini was sexy.
WALTER. See, I don't think so. She was very attractive. Stunning even. But sexy ... that's different.
TONY. So what do you think is sexy?
WALTER. Really? Okay ... well, it can be little things. Like when you see a woman wearing heels and she does that thing, where they tilt one foot back on the heel and kind of rock it from side to side.
NICK. What?
TONY. Yeah, I know what you mean. Like this. *(Tony demonstrates.)*
WALTER. Right.
TONY. Oh, yeah. I love that.
WALTER. Or that echo-y sound their heels make.
TONY. Yeah, that click-clack noise when they're walking down the street.
NICK. An echo is sexy?!
WALTER. Sure.
NICK. I think this woman headed this way in the pink one-piece with the cutouts is sexy. Am I right or not, Tony?
TONY. Hm? Oh ... yeah, she's a babe.
WALTER. So, what do you think is sexy, Tony?
TONY. Oh, you know ... lots of things.
WALTER. Like...?
TONY. ... nah, forget it.
NICK. Walt, get off it already.
WALTER. Nick, you wanted to talk about women, so we are. If you don't like it, why don't you run after that blonde, and tell her she only rated stunning instead of gorgeous because of the brown in her hair. I'm sure that'll get you laid. *(He turns back to Tony.)* So?
TONY. Ah, well ... I don't know, it's kind of weird.
NICK. Weirder than that heel thing?
TONY. No, I guess maybe not. I ... I kind of like when it's a little chilly out, like a cool spring night, and the women have dressed kinda light for the day, but at night they're cold ... and I think it's cute the way women cross their arms over their chests to stay warm. *(Slight pause.)* See? I told you it was weird.
NICK. What? I don't get that.
TONY. I don't know. It's just this thing women do that men don't.

NICK. Women do a lot of things men don't do.
WALTER. Well, that's it, isn't it. It's the differences that are sexy.
TONY. Yeah. Yeah, I think that's right.
NICK. I'm going for a swim.
TONY. No, wait. What do you think's sexy?
NICK. Oh, no. I'm not playing.
WALTER. Come on, Nick. Think about it.
NICK. *(Pause.)* Uh ... I don't know, but for some reason ... This is so stupid.
TONY. What?
NICK. *(Sighs.)* You know those things they put in their hair? To hold it back? The puffy things.
TONY. Scrunchies?
NICK. Yeah. Hair scrunchies.
WALTER. Why are those sexy?
NICK. I don't know. I just like to watch women put them in their hair. The way they run their fingers through their hair, and pull it back and wrap the scrunchy around.
TONY. Yeah, I can see that. *(There is a pause. The three men sit back and reflect for a moment.)*
NICK. And then sometimes, when you see a woman walking around with the scrunchy around her wrist. I love that.
TONY. Yeah, why is that? Why should that be sexy? *(Slight pause.)* Women get the best accessories.
WALTER. Yeah. Scrunchies are cool. *(There is another long pause.)*
NICK. You guys have ruined the beach for me. *(Blackout.)*

AUGUST

Heidi and Paige sit on a bench at the edge of a baseball diamond in a park. Ben stands nearby, swinging a softball bat. Phoebe paces in front of them, watching the game.

PHOEBE. *(Calling out to Elaine at home plate.)* No! Come on, Lainey! Keep your eye on the ball.
HEIDI. The shortstop is so cute.
PAIGE. I know, isn't he?
BEN. You think he's cute?
PAIGE. Are you kidding? Look at his ass. *(Ben looks at the shortstop, studying his ass. Phoebe watches Ben for a moment.)*
PHOEBE. Something you want to tell me, Ben?
BEN. What? Oh, no, I … was … Nothing.
PHOEBE. *(Calling to Elaine.)* Wait for your pitch!
HEIDI. *(To Phoebe.)* You're making her more nervous.
PHOEBE. Well, it's the last inning, and we need a run just to tie this thing. And she sucks! *(To Paige.)* Who's up next, Paige? You?
PAIGE. Ben's next. I'm after him.
PHOEBE. All right, good. People who can hit. Hey, ah … how's Wade?
PAIGE. Not good. I'm flying to L.A. to see him next week.
BEN. Looks like I'm up. *(Ben exits quickly as Elaine stomps into view, clearly unhappy.)*
ELAINE. I hate this game.
PAIGE. It was a good try. *(Elaine glares at her.)* Okay, well … I'm on deck. *(Paige exits.)*
HEIDI. *(Calling to Ben at home plate.)* All right, Ben. Get us on base!
PHOEBE. *(To Elaine.)* You're swinging too soon.
ELAINE. I don't care.
PHOEBE. You've gotta keep your eye on the ball.
ELAINE. What do you think I'm looking at?!
HEIDI. I've been looking at the shortstop.

ELAINE. Well, I wasn't.
PHOEBE. *(Calling to Ben.)* That's it, Ben. Wait for your pitch.
HEIDI. He's been watching you.
ELAINE. *(Slight pause.)* Really? *(Elaine looks out onto the field.)* Yeah, well, now his eyes are glued on Paige doing her stretches. I want her butt.
HEIDI. So does every guy on the field.

PHOEBE.	HEIDI.
Ben got a hit! Run! SAFE!	Run! He's safe! Yes!

ELAINE. Could it be any hotter? Why am I running around the park, when I should be hugging my air conditioner?
PHOEBE. *(Calling to Paige at home plate.)* All right, Paige. Bring him home.
ELAINE. *(Watching the game.)* Oh, would you look at that?! I didn't get pitches like that. They're serving her those on a tray. I got ones zipping at my head!
PHOEBE. Shut up. We need a hit.
ELAINE. Yeah, but those bastards are giving her easy ones because she's good-looking.
PHOEBE. Come on. You're both pretty.
ELAINE. Yeah, fine, I'm pretty. She's your basic thin-with-great-boobs-and-butt nightmare. The bitch.
PHOEBE. Hey!
ELAINE. Oh, it's not her. I just can't stand the way guys always go for the package. Why are men so obsessed with breasts? Do they know it's the same fat they hate everywhere else?
HEIDI. Hey, I like men.
ELAINE. I like men too. I just want to kill 'em sometimes.
HEIDI. *(Calling to home plate.)* Good eye, Paige. *(To Elaine.)* Not all men are bad, you know.
ELAINE. Not all cats shed.
PHOEBE. What cats don't shed?
ELAINE. Those ugly hairless ones. The sphinx, it's called. It's a mutation.
PHOEBE. That follows.
HEIDI. Oh, stop. Male bashing is just over already.
PHOEBE. And she should know. She got an "A" in her women's studies class at college.

HEIDI. Least I finished college.
PHOEBE. Hey!! That's unfair! I couldn't turn down a job like that! Right, Elaine?
ELAINE. Yeah. It was a great opportunity.
HEIDI. She hesitated.
ELAINE. No, I didn't.
PHOEBE. Actually, you did. Why was that?
ELAINE. Phoebe, this is stupid. Just drop it.
PHOEBE. No, you got something to say to me?
ELAINE. *(Slight pause, then in a rush.)* Well, you know, you're always talking about the one that got away. But if journalism was such a big thing for you, why didn't you find another job? It was like you expected something to just come and drop in your lap.
PHOEBE. What're you talking about? I did try! And there was that producer from the show who really wanted to take me with him to NBC.
ELAINE. Yeah, well, and maybe sleeping with him wasn't the best career move.
HEIDI. Whoa! News flash.
PHOEBE. Oh, that's real nice, coming from you, Elaine.
ELAINE. What's that supposed to mean?!
PHOEBE. Gee, I don't know, Miss "I'm Fucking a Married Man."
ELAINE. I can't even believe you said that!
PHOEBE. I called people, okay? I tried, but you get these jobs by who you know. I'm not connected anymore.
HEIDI. So get connected.
PHOEBE. Stay out of this, Heidi.
ELAINE. No. She's right. Find some job even if it's entry-level.
PHOEBE. I can't start at the bottom at thirty-three.
ELAINE. Well, you've got to do something, right? Or do you? You haven't worked since last spring. How's Ben feel about that?
PHOEBE. None of your damn business. Besides, no one hires over the summer.
HEIDI. I've got two job interviews next week.
PHOEBE. Oh, would you — ! You're kidding.
HEIDI. No. And I've got resumes out at some other places.
PHOEBE. No wonder Mom's giving me shit. I cannot fucking win.

ELAINE. You're not even trying.
PHOEBE. Elaine, back off, all right?!
ELAINE. Fine, whatever. It's your life. But your life's pretty good, by the way. You're married. Kids'll be next. I mean, you've got options you don't even see. Me? What've I got? I've got my job.
PHOEBE. You've got Walter.
ELAINE. Do I? I mean, he's still fighting with Nina over who gets the African masks and stuff. And I'm like, give her the damn masks and be done with it. If you want to be done with it. *(Paige jogs in.)*
PAIGE. Heidi, you're up.
HEIDI. I am? Oh! *(Heidi hurries off to bat.)*
PHOEBE. What happened? What did I miss?
PAIGE. I got a hit, moved Ben from first to third, but I got caught trying to make it to second.
PHOEBE. Two outs? Damn it.
PAIGE. And you're up next.
PHOEBE. Okay, Heidi, wait for … Oh, just go for it! *(Slight pause.)* Lainey, I'm sorry I … I'm sorry. But listen, I see the way Walter looks at you. Give it time. *(Slight pause.)* Pretend you're in a plane that's crashing …
ELAINE. What? Oh, just go end this game, so we can get out of here. *(Phoebe hurries off.)*
PAIGE. Yeah, Heidi! Run! All right! Nice hit.
ELAINE. Well, he may have a great ass, but the shortstop blew that play.
PAIGE. Okay, show 'em how it's done, Phoebe! *(To Elaine.)* So, hey … how's Walter?
ELAINE. He's okay. He's good.
PAIGE. Yeah? He's a great guy. Have you met his brother?
ELAINE. Yeah, we went to some awful movie with Nick a couple weeks ago.
PAIGE. Oh, Nicky likes the worst movies. *(Slight pause.)* How's he doing, do you know?
ELAINE. He's all right, I guess.
PAIGE. Yeah? *(Slight pause.)* Is he seeing anyone?
ELAINE. Uh … I don't know. *(Slight pause.)* Why?
PAIGE. Oh, you know, just … curious. Just wondering if … If.
ELAINE. Yeah. I know.

PHOEBE. *(Offstage.)* NOOOOO!
PAIGE. Oh jeez, what happened?
ELAINE. *(Smiling.)* Phoebe struck out. *(Blackout.)*

SEPTEMBER

A kitchen. Gwen and Chris enter carrying dirty dishes.

GWEN. She wants something.
CHRIS. What?
GWEN. She wants something.
CHRIS. What makes you say that?
GWEN. She's here, isn't she?
CHRIS. Because I invited her.
GWEN. Who called who?
CHRIS. *(Slight pause.)* What difference does that make?
GWEN. I knew it.
CHRIS. Oh, you always think Phoebe's plotting something.
GWEN. She usually is.
CHRIS. And you're on to her, but poor Dad is just wrapped around her little finger, huh?
GWEN. Well, you are, Chris.
CHRIS. Oh, that's not true at all. I think she's upset. She didn't even finish her chocolate cake. Something's wrong.
GWEN. Like what?
CHRIS. Well, I don't know, but why isn't Ben here? I invited them both over for dinner.
GWEN. She said why.
CHRIS. He's tired and just wanted to go home and listen to some new record he bought? I don't buy that.
GWEN. You're reading into things. They just moved. Ben probably just wants to get settled.
CHRIS. I'm telling you, she's upset.
GWEN. Yes, I can tell by her red-rimmed eyes.

CHRIS. Just because she doesn't wail and moan doesn't mean she's not worried. It's subtle.
GWEN. That's how I know. If something was really wrong she'd tell us. Or you. But she is being subtle. Now, you may read that as being upset, but I know she's maneuvering for position.
CHRIS. And what if she does want something?
GWEN. Then she's out of luck.
CHRIS. Why?
GWEN. Because.
CHRIS. Because?
GWEN. Yes. Because we did our job, you know. She left the nest. We don't have to keep stuffing grubs into her mouth. She's supposed to find her own grubs now.
CHRIS. That's a warm, fuzzy vision of parenthood.
GWEN. Well, we didn't get constant propping up from our parents. Why should she?
CHRIS. It was a different time.
GWEN. It's always a different time. *(Slight pause.)* If just once she'd finish something she started I'd feel differently. But she trails unfinished projects and jobs behind her like bread crumbs. And then when she's out of dough she comes flying back home.
CHRIS. I think you're mixing your metaphors there.
GWEN. You always try to change the argument to something else when you don't want to deal with what's at hand.
CHRIS. No, I don't. How can you say that?
GWEN. See? Now we're fighting about this instead of what I said.
CHRIS. Fine, fine. But I don't think you're being fair. No, she hasn't succeeded in everything, but I'm proud of the way she's always trying new things.
GWEN. Of course she is. Because she never just bears down and sticks to something. *(Slight pause.)* Look, Chris, we're only a few years away from retirement. Phoebe's married. Heidi graduated. She's getting a job. This is when our responsibilities end, isn't it? It's a cliché, but isn't this supposed to be our time?
CHRIS. How will it not be our time if Phoebe needs some help with something? We're well-provided financially.
GWEN. *(Slight pause.)* I'm tired of being a parent, okay? Thirty-plus years of my life has been quite enough. I want to be the focus

of my own life for a while. *(Pause.)* Look, Chris, I don't want to see her unhappy or struggling. You know that. But she's got to see there comes a time when you realize that you can't have everything you want. You have to compromise.
CHRIS. *(Slight pause.)* Gwen, I ... I know what you're saying, but ... I don't know. *(Phoebe enters carrying some other plates.)*
PHOEBE. I called Ben. He says hi.
CHRIS. How is he?
PHOEBE. He's fine.
CHRIS. Well, good. Good. So, how's the new apartment?
PHOEBE. Oh, it's great. *(Slight pause.)* I mean, you know, there's little things. Ben's taken over part of our bedroom with some posters and things I could live without. But I know he hates that old clock of Grandma's that always rings the wrong number of times. So, it's a compromise, right?
GWEN. Yes, indeed.
PHOEBE. Listen, I had something I wanted to ask you guys.
GWEN. Really?
CHRIS. Gwen.
PHOEBE. What's going on?
CHRIS. Nothing. So, what's wrong?
PHOEBE. Nothing's wrong. What's up with you two?
CHRIS. Nothing.
GWEN. What did you want to ask?
PHOEBE. Well, lately I've been reevaluating things. Everyone I know has a real career. Ben with architecture, Elaine's at Random House. But I've let myself kind of drift. Which I'm sure you'll agree with, Mom.
CHRIS. And so what have you been thinking?
PHOEBE. *(Pause.)* I want to go back to school. *(Slight pause.)* I want to finish college and then go on to graduate school in journalism. I talked with the admissions office up at Columbia, and if I hurry and get my application in now I can be considered for the spring semester.
CHRIS. Wow. What brought this on?
PHOEBE. Well, Heidi's graduation got me thinking, but ... it's kind of dumb, but I was filling out this questionnaire recently, and there was this section that asked about your education, and I'm

sick of checking the box that says, "some college education." I mean, I did well in school. It's not like it was too hard for me.
CHRIS. I don't know if that's the best reason to go back to school.
PHOEBE. That's not the reason, Dad.
CHRIS. You shouldn't feel you have to do this because of Heidi either.
PHOEBE. No, Dad … this is about me.
CHRIS. How many more credits do you need to finish?
PHOEBE. I missed senior year. But if I get admitted for the spring, I can get all my course work done by working through the spring and summer, and go straight into grad school next fall.
CHRIS. That's an awful lot of work
PHOEBE. That's why I kept putting it off. Every time I thought about it, it seemed more daunting. But I need to do this.
CHRIS. What does Ben think of this?
PHOEBE. He's being … pretty supportive.
GWEN. How much money do you need?
PHOEBE. Uh … yeah, well, that's what I … It depends on how much I can get in financial aid. But … I think I may need another three or four thousand. Each semester.
GWEN. *(Long pause.)* Well, I think we can do that. Don't you, Chris?
CHRIS. Huh? Oh. Yeah, sure.
PHOEBE. Really?
GWEN. Yes. I think it's a wonderful idea.
PHOEBE. Oh, my God! I didn't think it would be this easy. Oh, my God! Thank you! Thank you! *(Phoebe hugs Gwen tightly.)*
GWEN. Well … what are parents for?
PHOEBE. Wow, I … I've got to call Ben! *(She hurries out of the kitchen. Chris stares at Gwen, who busies herself with dishes or something on the countertop. Finally, she turns to him.)*
GWEN. What?
CHRIS. You old softy, you.
GWEN. I am not. I'm just glad she's finally getting her degree. I mean, it's years too late, but — *(Chris folds his arms around her and kisses her cheek.)*
CHRIS. You don't fool me.
GWEN. *(Pause.)* Well, don't tell her. *(Blackout.)*

OCTOBER

A living room. Ben searches for something under the couch. The doorbell rings, and Ben gets up and opens the door. Walter enters.

WALTER. Ben, are you okay?
BEN. Oh, I'm glad you're here, Walter.
WALTER. Elaine just called me. She says Phoebe's at her place crying ... saying she left you.
BEN. Can you help me with something?
WALTER. Yeah, of course.
BEN. Go into the other room and look under the bed. Tell me if you see anything. *(Ben searches the couch's cushions. Walter is confused, but hurries offstage to the bedroom.)*
WALTER. *(Offstage.)* Ah ... I had no idea things between you two were bad.
BEN. That's just it. Things have been great. This came out of nowhere. I mean, we're having a little fight ... and the next thing I know she's packing her bags and she's out the door. *(Slight pause.)* Do you see anything? *(Walter returns.)*
WALTER. No, just dust. *(Slight pause.)* So ... what did you argue about?
BEN. It's silly when you look at it. *(Slight pause.)* We fought about the Beatles.
WALTER. *(Pause.)* John, Paul, George and Ringo?
BEN. Yeah. She says I'm too obsessed with the Beatles.
WALTER. What?
BEN. Yeah, can you believe that?
WALTER. What do you mean by obsessed?
BEN. Thank you! That's what I said.
WALTER. No ... how did the fight start?
BEN. She broke my Yellow Submarine.
WALTER. Yeah, so? Buy a new CD.

BEN. No, not the album. My Yellow Submarine. The Corgi die-cast metal toy manufactured in 1968 and released with the animated movie.
WALTER. Oh, right. A friend of mine had one of those when I was a kid. So ... Phoebe broke it?
BEN. She was vacuuming and knocked it off its shelf. I came home and found it on the floor with some paint chipped off.
WALTER. *(Pause.)* Is that all?
BEN. All?! No, that's not all! John and Paul fell out of the sub, and ... and I think she vacuumed them up! She'd already thrown out the garbage, so I ran down to the street, but the trash had been picked up. I've been looking all over the apartment, just in case ... but nothing.
WALTER. *(Slight pause.)* What fell out?
BEN. John and Paul! There's a button on the side, and when you press it a hatch opens and —
WALTER. John and Paul pop out.
BEN. Right. So, I mean I guess I kind of lost my temper and said, "How could you do that? You've got to be more careful around my Beatles case."
WALTER. Ben, it was just an accident.
BEN. I know, I know. You should have heard her. "I'm sorry. But you don't have to make me feel so bad. Sometimes I think you care more about your stupid Beatles than me."
WALTER. And what did you say?
BEN. "Are you calling the people who created *Sgt. Pepper's Lonely Hearts Club Band* stupid?! Are you insane?!"
WALTER. How could you say that?!
BEN. She lost John and Paul!
WALTER. It's just a toy!
BEN. Toy, hell. I paid four hundred dollars for that submarine. Now it's chipped and John and Paul are gone. That drops the price to a hundred and fifty dollars at most.
WALTER. Are you kidding me?
BEN. Who'd want a Yellow Submarine without John and Paul?
WALTER. You paid four hundred dollars for an old toy?
BEN. It's a collector's item.
WALTER. Who pays that much for a toy that isn't two hundred years old?

BEN. Beatles collectors.
WALTER. *(Pause.)* All right, leaving that aside for a moment ... she says, you care for the Beatles more than her. You call her crazy ... and then what happened?
BEN. She ran out of the room crying.
WALTER. Please tell me you went after her.
BEN. Well, I ... I wanted to. But ... I had to go downstairs to check the garbage.
WALTER. Oh, yes. Of course.
BEN. But when I got back up here and saw she was packing, I got very emotional, really upset.
WALTER. All right, good. I hope you told her you were sorry.
BEN. Yeah, of course. I apologized over and over. And I said, "Please don't go. Today of all days."
WALTER. Uh-huh, and ... "Today of all days"?
BEN. It's October ninth. John Lennon's birthday. I always like to light a candle, have some wine and listen to *Abbey Road* or something. She knows what that means to me.
WALTER. Every year?
BEN. Yeah, and this year's special because I just took all my Beatles collectibles out of storage.
WALTER. Yeah, I noticed. There's Beatles stuff all over your bedroom.
BEN. Well, I decided, this is part of who I am, you know. And what's the point in having these things if they're not out where you can enjoy them?
WALTER. But do you really need two display cases of ... I don't know what.
BEN. Aren't those great? They're arranged chronologically, so the first case has memorabilia from 1960 to '65. There's Beatle bubble bath and beach towels, hair cream, tour programs, even panty hose. Then the second case goes from '66 to 1970, so it's got a lot of Yellow Submarine stuff, like puzzles and stationery. I've even got two lunchboxes. With no rust on them at all.
WALTER. *(Slight pause.)* Ben ... have you been drinking?
BEN. What? No!
WALTER. Well, Phoebe's right.
BEN. About what?

WALTER. Look, I love the Beatles too, but ... I mean, Phoebe just left you and all you can talk about is the Fab Four.
BEN. That's what the whole argument was about.
WALTER. No, the fight was about the fact that you're obsessed with a band that broke up in 1969.
BEN. 1970.
WALTER. My point exactly!
BEN. What are you saying?
WALTER. You need a little help from your friends.
BEN. *(Pause.)* Oh, that's not fair.
WALTER. No? Then how 'bout "all you need is love"?
BEN. *(Pause.)* Right. Okay, yeah, you're right. Of course. Thank you.
WALTER. Any time. "I am you, as you are me, and we are all together."
BEN. What?
WALTER. From "I Am the Walrus." "I am you, as you are me, and we are all together."
BEN. No. It's "I am *he,* as you are me." Not "I am you." *(Slight pause.)* Get out of my house.
WALTER. Ben —
BEN. NO! You can call me crazy, you can take Phoebe's side, but when you twist the words of the Beatles to suit your own purposes, that's when I want you out.
WALTER. Okay, shut up and listen! *(Slight pause.)* You think marriage is tough? You think trying to live with another person — love their good points and accept their failings — is hard? Try divorce. *(Slight pause.)* I know what you're going through. You get married and things are great. You and Phoebe are happy. But then you start to disagree about money or when to have kids, and suddenly everything's a problem. Everyone says marriage isn't easy, but you didn't think it would be this hard, did you? *(Slight pause.)* Well, let me tell you ... divorce ... that's something that most mornings you wake up and wonder if this'll be the day it all becomes too much, and you decide to step out that tenth floor window. *(Slight pause.)* So, you need to dig down in yourself and decide what it is you want in your life. And if Phoebe is something you want ... then you're going to have to do some hard work. *(Pause.)* Do you know what you want?

BEN. *(Pause.)* You said Phoebe's at Elaine's?
WALTER. Yeah. *(Ben gets to his feet and quickly exits. Walter, worn out, sits. Blackout.)*

NOVEMBER

A hotel room. Phoebe is on the telephone. Ben sits at a table, writing on a pad of paper.

PHOEBE. Okay, Mom. I'll call you when we're back in New York. *(She hangs up and Ben turns to her.)*
BEN. How's this: *(Reading from the pad and going from memory.)* Wade and I became friends when we were fifteen and met during our fourth period theater class in tenth grade. Over the next few months as we became best friends, I remember thinking I couldn't wait until we were thirty so I could say I'd known him for half my life. *(Slight pause.)* Well, I'm past thirty now, but I feel like I've known him all my life. And in a way, I think I have and always will, despite what the calendar may try to say. *(Slight pause.)*

Because I live in New York and he lived in Los Angeles, Wade and I could sometimes go months without talking or over a year without seeing each other. But we always picked up right where we left off, like we saw each other everyday. We could spontaneously break into scenes from *Monty Python and the Holy Grail*. Much to the dismay of those around us. Time and distance didn't seem to affect our relationship. *(Slight pause.)*

Which was good because Wade was always on the go … working … traveling. But that was Wade. He could never sit still for too long. I used to feel lazy next to him. He had such drive and energy, he was always moving from one project right into the next. And when he learned he was HIV-positive, it was natural for him to become an activist and scholar where the disease was concerned, while still giving his all to his work at the museum. *(Pause.)*

It was very important to Phoebe and me that Wade was able

to be a part of our wedding last summer. Wade never let an opportunity pass without telling me he thought she was terrific, and she felt the same about him. And the three of us always had a great time together, be it visiting the stark Joshua Tree National Park or going to Seventies disco night at the Apache Club, a gay bar in L.A., where both Wade and Phoebe were asked to dance, and I, unaccountably, was not. *(Pause.)*

I know there will always be things I want to share with Wade, but won't be able to now. Even in the past three days there have been things he would have gotten a kick out of. *(Slight pause.)* Not a half hour after he died, for instance. Phoebe and I were with him and his family in the hospital. It was a little after seven-thirty. After crying and hugging the others, Phoebe and I went out into the hall. A few minutes later Paige, Wade's sister, came out, leaving her parents alone with him. And the three of us are sitting there on the floor of the hospital corridor, still crying ... when at eight o'clock a voice comes over the P.A. system to announce ... "Visiting hours are now over." *(Slight pause.)* Which just seemed hysterical to me, and I'm trying not to laugh, but I see Phoebe giggling quietly and Paige smiling. Seeing each other we all burst out laughing. *(Pause.)*

Later that night back at the hotel, I dialed Wade's number to leave Paige a message, and I was so startled to hear his voice on the answering machine I couldn't remember why I called. Then Phoebe and I called back just so we could hear Wade one last time. *(Slight pause.)*

You know, when a person dies I think it's the sound of their voice we miss the most. The face is so often captured in a photograph, but the voice is a rare thing. And it's really the voice that defines a person, because it's through their voice we come to know their thoughts and feelings, everything about them. So to miss the sound of a voice is to miss the very being of that person. *(Pause.)*

We're gathered here because we were lucky enough to have had Wade in our lives. We were all touched by his intelligence, his humor, compassion and vitality. And despite the pain we now feel, how much poorer would our lives be if we couldn't think of him and say, "He was my son," or "He was my brother," or "He was

my friend"?
PHOEBE. *(Pause.)* That's beautiful.
BEN. Thank you. *(They hug one another tightly. Fade to black.)*

DECEMBER

An airport terminal. Walter enters, with a backpack slung over his shoulder, and crosses to an empty row of chairs. He sits down and stretches his legs out. A moment later, Nick struggles on with a backpack and two large, overstuffed bags. Walter does not lift a finger to help. Nick drops his bags and sits.

WALTER. They're never going to let you on the plane with all that.
NICK. I'll get on.
WALTER. There's a limit for carry-on luggage. You're going to have to check those.
NICK. Let me worry about it, okay?
WALTER. I'm just trying to save you some —
NICK. Save it, period! *(Nick rummages through one of his bags and pulls out a magazine to read. Walter just watches him.)* Don't you have a book to read or something?
WALTER. No.
NICK. Well, I'll watch your seat if you wanna go get one. There was a gift shop back there.
WALTER. No, I'm fine. *(Nick goes back to his magazine. Walter looks over Nick's bags.)*
NICK. What?
WALTER. Nothing.
NICK. No. Why are you staring at my stuff?
WALTER. I'm just wondering what you've got there. We're just going for a few days. How much of your wardrobe did you bring?
NICK. It's mostly presents.
WALTER. You're kidding.

NICK. My clothes are in here. The other two are presents. Why?
WALTER. Both those bags are just presents?
NICK. Yeah.
WALTER. For Mom and Dad and me?
NICK. Well, mostly for Mom and Dad.
WALTER. Oh, well, sure. *(Pause.)* What gives?
NICK. Walt, what are you getting at? It's Christmas. Like many families we have this odd tradition of exchanging gifts.
WALTER. Not you.
NICK. Excuse me?
WALTER. You don't go in for big gift giving.
NICK. I give plenty of gifts.
WALTER. You buy nice presents, but you're always pretty restrained with the number.
NICK. Are you saying I'm cheap?
WALTER. No, that's not it.
NICK. Because I can easily return the things I got you.
WALTER. Things? Plural?
NICK. Knock it off!
WALTER. Nick, you just don't normally do all this.
NICK. Please go get something to read.
WALTER. I'm not trying to get on your case. I'm just curious.
NICK. Look, I just picked up a few more presents this year.
WALTER. So you admit that —
NICK. Yes, yes, fine!! I'm cheap. Can we drop this now?!
WALTER. *(Pause.)* So what made you get more this year?
NICK. So help me, Walt ...
WALTER. Do you feel guilty about something?
NICK. Don't you analyze me.
WALTER. I'm sorry. I don't mean to. Really. *(Slight pause.)* But if I pick up on this, don't you think Mom and Dad will?
NICK. *(Pause.)* Shit.
WALTER. So, what's up?
NICK. I just ... I don't know how to talk with them anymore.
WALTER. About what?
NICK. About personal stuff. Life. Do you still wonder what they think about the things you do, the people you see?
WALTER. Of course. Hell, it took me almost a month to tell

them about me and Nina splitting up. I just couldn't face them. And when I did, I told them it was mutual.
NICK. Why?
WALTER. I didn't want them to think badly of her.
NICK. She had an affair on you. They should think badly of her.
WALTER. Yeah, but ... I thought it reflected on me.
NICK. Oh, no. Mom and Dad wouldn't think that way.
WALTER. Come on. How long have they been married? Nina and I were married for, what, not quite four years, and it's over. Of course they're going to wonder what I did wrong.
NICK. Yeah, they've been together a long time. That's why they'd understand. I don't think you stay together that long without going through some stuff. And if they did wonder, they'd just blame it on her.
WALTER. Well, I didn't want that. I mean, they liked her so much.
NICK. No, they didn't. None of us did.
WALTER. What?
NICK. Mom and Dad thought she was okay, I guess, but not a lot. And I never liked her.
WALTER. You're kidding. Why?
NICK. Oh, it's just ... she was such a bitch.
WALTER. Excuse me?!
NICK. Man, that feels good to say.
WALTER. Why didn't you tell me?
NICK. Oh, come on. What was I supposed to do? "Oh, Walt, I know you're totally drooling over this woman and you're planning to marry her, but I think she's a harpy." Yeah, that'd go over real well.
WALTER. Why didn't you like her?
NICK. She was pretentious. And she made you pretentious. *(Walter is silent. Nick watches him.)* Have you told them about Elaine?
WALTER. Sort of. I've told them I've been dating someone. I just haven't told them we see so much of each other we're practically living together.
NICK. Why not?
WALTER. It's just ... I mean, come on, my divorce isn't even finalized yet. I don't want them thinking I'm making a mistake.
NICK. Hey, parents are supposed to worry. That's their job, right?

WALTER. *(Slight pause.)* I think she wanted to come.
NICK. Elaine?
WALTER. Yeah. I think she hoped I'd invite her down for Christmas.
NICK. You should have. If only to have someone besides Mom and Dad to talk to. Hell, if I'd been dating anyone for more than a week I'd have brought her along. After more than a day or two with them I'm totally burned out. You need a good excuse to get out of the house
WALTER. Yeah, it's like the roof will cave in if we have five minutes of silence.
NICK. *(Pause.)* So, why didn't you invite her?
WALTER. It just feels complicated. Last Christmas I fly down with my wife, this year I bring my lover.
NICK. Hey, at least you got married. I couldn't even manage that.
WALTER. *(Pause.)* Is that why you got so many presents?
NICK. You're not gonna let this go, are you? Okay, yeah. Probably. I just don't want to talk to them about it.
WALTER. Okay. So talk to me.
NICK. Oh, come on …
WALTER. No, really.
NICK. I can't.
WALTER. Why not?
NICK. What, I'm supposed to whine about getting dumped to someone whose wife has been screwing around?
WALTER. You're supposed to whine to your brother.
NICK. It wouldn't feel right.
WALTER. Why not?
NICK. Because we don't get along.
WALTER. Yeah, we do.
NICK. Since when? We're totally different. We almost never hang out together, and when we do we either talk about the weather or we argue.
WALTER. We don't have to like the same things to like each other.
NICK. How can people not like the same things, but like each other? I don't even like people who don't like the Yankees.
WALTER. *(Pause.)* Do you like me?
NICK. Ah, damn it. Why didn't you bring a book?!

WALTER. Nick?
NICK. Why are you doing this?
WALTER. Because I love you.
NICK. *(Pause.)* Shit.
WALTER. *(Slight pause.)* You don't have to say anything. I'm sorry. *(Pause.)* Watch my seat, will you? I'm gonna get something to read. *(Walter gets to his feet.)*
NICK. Wait. *(He reaches into one of his bags and pulls out a wrapped gift.)* Here.
WALTER. Thank you.
NICK. It's a book.
WALTER. Thanks. I'd give you something, but I mailed all the boxes to Charleston.
NICK. Boxes? Plural?
WALTER. Yeah. Five.
NICK. You sent five boxes and you gave me shit about "why so many presents"?
WALTER. Just trying to annoy you.
NICK. Well, good work. Thanks. *(Walter tears open the wrapping on the present.)*
WALTER. *The House That Ruth Built: A History of the New York Yankees.*
NICK. You can return it.
WALTER. Why?
NICK. Well, it's baseball.
WALTER. Hey, I love the Yankees.
NICK. Really?
WALTER. Sure. Who doesn't?
FLIGHT ATTENDANT'S VOICE. *(Over the P.A. system.)* Ladies and gentlemen, flight 463 for Charleston is now ready for boarding. We'll begin by boarding rows twenty-five and higher. Please have your boarding passes ready for the gate attendant. Due to federal regulations only one piece of carry-on luggage will be allowed.
NICK. Damn it.
WALTER. Here, I'll take one.
NICK. Yeah? Thanks.
WALTER. No problem. Let's go.
NICK. You should call Elaine. Ask her to catch the next flight

down. Call her from the plane. Women love that.
WALTER. I just might.
NICK. Ask her if she's got any cute friends who're alone this Christmas.
WALTER. You're always thinking of others. You're such a saint.
NICK. That's me. Saint Nick. *(They pick up the bags and walk out. Blackout.)*

End of Play

PROPERTY LIST

Glass of champagne (ELAINE)
Purse (ELAINE)
Kleenex (ELAINE)
Coffee cups (PHOEBE, BEN)
Bride's magazines (PHOEBE)
Cell phone (TONY)
Wallet containing scrap of paper (TONY)
Flashlight (PAIGE)
Sieve (PAIGE)
Glasses of wine (PHOEBE, ELAINE)
Video camera (PHOEBE)
Bag (ELAINE)
Gift-wrapped pair of earrings (ELAINE)
Note cards (HEIDI)
Lipstick case (PHOEBE)
Blue garter (ELAINE)
Boutonniere (GWEN)
Bouquet (PHOEBE)
Paperback book (WALTER)
Softball bat (BEN)
Dirty dishes (GWEN, CHRIS, PHOEBE)
Telephone (PHOEBE)
Pad of paper and writing utensil (BEN)
Backpack (WALTER, NICK)
Two large bags (NICK)
Magazine (NICK)
Gift-wrapped book (NICK)

SOUND EFFECTS

New Year's Eve party
Phone ringing
Crash of kitchen utensils
"Pomp and Circumstance"
Doorbell
Voice-over

NEW PLAYS

★ **THE EXONERATED by Jessica Blank and Erik Jensen.** Six interwoven stories paint a picture of an American criminal justice system gone horribly wrong and six brave souls who persevered to survive it. "The #1 play of the year…intense and deeply affecting…" –*NY Times*. "Riveting. Simple, honest storytelling that demands reflection." –*A.P.* "Artful and moving…pays tribute to the resilience of human hearts and minds." –*Variety*. "Stark…riveting…cunningly orchestrated." –*The New Yorker*. "Hard-hitting, powerful, and socially relevant." –*Hollywood Reporter*. [7M, 3W] ISBN: 0-8222-1946-8

★ **STRING FEVER by Jacquelyn Reingold.** Lily juggles the big issues: turning forty, artificial insemination and the elusive scientific Theory of Everything in this Off-Broadway comedy hit. "Applies the elusive rules of string theory to the conundrums of one woman's love life. Think *Sex and the City* meets *Copenhagen*." –*NY Times*. "A funny offbeat and touching look at relationships…an appealing romantic comedy populated by oddball characters." –*NY Daily News*. "Where kooky, zany, and madcap meet…whimsically winsome." –*NY Magazine*. "STRING FEVER will have audience members happily stringing along." –*TheaterMania.com*. "Reingold's language is surprising, inventive, and unique." –*nytheatre.com*. "…[a] whimsical comic voice." –*Time Out*. [3M, 3W (doubling)] ISBN: 0-8222-1952-2

★ **DEBBIE DOES DALLAS adapted by Erica Schmidt, composed by Andrew Sherman, conceived by Susan L. Schwartz.** A modern morality tale told as a comic musical of tragic proportions as the classic film is brought to the stage. "A scream! A saucy, tongue-in-cheek romp." –*The New Yorker*. "Hilarious! DEBBIE manages to have it all: beauty, brains and a great sense of humor!" –*Time Out*. "Shamelessly silly, shrewdly self-aware and proud of being naughty. Great fun!" –*NY Times*. "Racy and raucous, a lighthearted, fast-paced thoroughly engaging and hilarious send-up." –*NY Daily News*. [3M, 5W] ISBN: 0-8222-1955-7

★ **THE MYSTERY PLAYS by Roberto Aguirre-Sacasa.** Two interrelated one acts, loosely based on the tradition of the medieval mystery plays. "… stylish, spine-tingling…Mr. Aguirre-Sacasa uses standard tricks of horror stories, borrowing liberally from masters like Kafka, Lovecraft, Hitchcock…But his mastery of the genre is his own…irresistible." –*NY Times*. "Undaunted by the special-effects limitations of theatre, playwright and *Marvel* comic-book writer Roberto Aguirre-Sacasa maps out some creepy twilight zones in THE MYSTERY PLAYS, an engaging, related pair of one acts…The theatre may rarely deliver shocks equivalent to, say, *Dawn of the Dead*, but Aguirre-Sacasa's work is fine compensation." –*Time Out*. [4M, 2W] ISBN: 0-8222-2038-5

★ **THE JOURNALS OF MIHAIL SEBASTIAN by David Auburn.** This epic one-man play spans eight tumultuous years and opens a uniquely personal window on the Romanian Holocaust and the Second World War. "Powerful." –*NY Times*. "[THE JOURNALS OF MIHAIL SEBASTIAN] allows us to glimpse the idiosyncratic effects of that awful history on one intelligent, pragmatic, recognizably real man…" –*NY Newsday*. [3M, 5W] ISBN: 0-8222-2006-7

★ **LIVING OUT by Lisa Loomer.** The story of the complicated relationship between a Salvadoran nanny and the Anglo lawyer she works for. "A stellar new play. Searingly funny." –*The New Yorker*. "Both generous and merciless, equally enjoyable and disturbing." –*NY Newsday*. "A bitingly funny new comedy. The plight of working mothers is explored from two pointedly contrasting perspectives in this sympathetic, sensitive new play." –*Variety*. [2M, 6W] ISBN: 0-8222-1994-8

DRAMATISTS PLAY SERVICE, INC.
440 Park Avenue South, New York, NY 10016   212-683-8960   Fax 212-213-1539
postmaster@dramatists.com   www.dramatists.com

NEW PLAYS

★ **MATCH by Stephen Belber.** Mike and Lisa Davis interview a dancer and choreographer about his life, but it is soon evident that their agenda will either ruin or inspire them—and definitely change their lives forever. "Prolific laughs and ear-to-ear smiles." –*NY Magazine*. "Uproariously funny, deeply moving, enthralling theater. Stephen Belber's MATCH has great beauty and tenderness, and abounds in wit." –*NY Daily News*. "Three and a half out of four stars." –*USA Today*. "A theatrical steeplechase that leads straight from outrageous bitchery to unadorned, heartfelt emotion." –*Wall Street Journal*. [2M, 1W] ISBN: 0-8222-2020-2

★ **HANK WILLIAMS: LOST HIGHWAY by Randal Myler and Mark Harelik.** The story of the beloved and volatile country-music legend Hank Williams, featuring twenty-five of his most unforgettable songs. "[LOST HIGHWAY has] the exhilarating feeling of Williams on stage in a particular place on a particular night…serves up classic country with the edges raw and the energy hot…By the end of the play, you've traveled on a profound emotional journey: LOST HIGHWAY transports its audience and communicates the inspiring message of the beauty and richness of Williams' songs…forceful, clear-eyed, moving, impressive." –*Rolling Stone*. "…honors a very particular musical talent with care and energy… smart, sweet, poignant." –*NY Times*. [7M, 3W] ISBN: 0-8222-1985-9

★ **THE STORY by Tracey Scott Wilson.** An ambitious black newspaper reporter goes against her editor to investigate a murder and finds the *best* story…but at what cost? "A singular new voice…deeply emotional, deeply intellectual, and deeply musical…" –*The New Yorker*. "…a conscientious and absorbing new drama…" –*NY Times*. "…a riveting, tough-minded drama about race, reporting and the truth…" –*A.P.* "… a stylish, attention-holding script that ends on a chilling note that will leave viewers with much to talk about." –*Curtain Up*. [2M, 7W (doubling, flexible casting)] ISBN: 0-8222-1998-0

★ **OUR LADY OF 121st STREET by Stephen Adly Guirgis.** The body of Sister Rose, beloved Harlem nun, has been stolen, reuniting a group of life-challenged childhood friends who square off as they wait for her return. "A scorching and dark new comedy… Mr. Guirgis has one of the finest imaginations for dialogue to come along in years." –*NY Times*. "Stephen Guirgis may be the best playwright in America under forty." –*NY Magazine*. [8M, 4W] ISBN: 0-8222-1965-4

★ **HOLLYWOOD ARMS by Carrie Hamilton and Carol Burnett.** The coming-of-age story of a dreamer who manages to escape her bleak life and follow her romantic ambitions to stardom. Based on Carol Burnett's bestselling autobiography, *One More Time*. "…pure theatre and pure entertainment…" –*Talkin' Broadway*. "…a warm, fuzzy evening of theatre." –*BrodwayBeat.com*. "…chuckles and smiles of recognition or surprise flow naturally…a remarkable slice of life." –*TheatreScene.net*. [5M, 5W, 1 girl] ISBN: 0-8222-1959-X

★ **INVENTING VAN GOGH by Steven Dietz.** A haunting and hallucinatory drama about the making of art, the obsession to create and the fine line that separates truth from myth. "Like a van Gogh painting, Dietz's story is a gorgeous example of excess—one that remakes reality with broad, well-chosen brush strokes. At evening's end, we're left with the author's resounding opinions on art and artifice, and provoked by his constant query into which is greater: van Gogh's art or his violent myth." –*Phoenix New Times*. "Dietz's writing is never simple. It is always brilliant. Shaded, compressed, direct, lucid—he frames his subject with a remarkable understanding of painting as a physical experience." –*Tucson Citizen*. [4M, 1W] ISBN: 0-8222-1954-9

DRAMATISTS PLAY SERVICE, INC.
440 Park Avenue South, New York, NY 10016 212-683-8960 Fax 212-213-1539
postmaster@dramatists.com   www.dramatists.com

NEW PLAYS

★ **INTIMATE APPAREL by Lynn Nottage.** The moving and lyrical story of a turn-of-the-century black seamstress whose gifted hands and sewing machine are the tools she uses to fashion her dreams from the whole cloth of her life's experiences. "...Nottage's play has a delicacy and eloquence that seem absolutely right for the time she is depicting..." –*NY Daily News*. "...thoughtful, affecting...The play offers poignant commentary on an era when the cut and color of one's dress—and of course, skin—determined whom one could and could not marry, sleep with, even talk to in public." –*Variety*. [2M, 4W] ISBN: 0-8222-2009-1

★ **BROOKLYN BOY by Donald Margulies.** A witty and insightful look at what happens to a writer when his novel hits the bestseller list. "The characters are beautifully drawn, the dialogue sparkles..." –*nytheatre.com*. "Few playwrights have the mastery to smartly investigate so much through a laugh-out-loud comedy that combines the vintage subject matter of successful writer-returning-to-ethnic-roots with the familiar mid-life crisis." –*Show Business Weekly*. [4M, 3W] ISBN: 0-8222-2074-1

★ **CROWNS by Regina Taylor.** Hats become a springboard for an exploration of black history and identity in this celebratory musical play. "Taylor pulls off a Hat Trick: She scores thrice, turning CROWNS into an artful amalgamation of oral history, fashion show, and musical theater..." –*TheatreMania.com*. "...wholly theatrical...Ms. Taylor has created a show that seems to arise out of spontaneous combustion, as if a bevy of department-store customers simultaneously decided to stage a revival meeting in the changing room." –*NY Times*. [1M, 6W (2 musicians)] ISBN: 0-8222-1963-8

★ **EXITS AND ENTRANCES by Athol Fugard.** The story of a relationship between a young playwright on the threshold of his career and an aging actor who has reached the end of his. "[Fugard] can say more with a single line than most playwrights convey in an entire script...Paraphrasing the title, it's safe to say this drama, making its memorable entrance into our consciousness, is unlikely to exit as long as a theater exists for exceptional work." –*Variety*. "A thought-provoking, elegant and engrossing new play..." –*Hollywood Reporter*. [2M] ISBN: 0-8222-2041-5

★ **BUG by Tracy Letts.** A thriller featuring a pair of star-crossed lovers in an Oklahoma City motel facing a bug invasion, paranoia, conspiracy theories and twisted psychological motives. "...obscenely exciting...top-flight craftsmanship. Buckle up and brace yourself..." –*NY Times*. "...[a] thoroughly outrageous and thoroughly entertaining play...the possibility of enemies, real and imagined, to squash has never been more theatrical." –*A.P.* [3M, 2W] ISBN: 0-8222-2016-4

★ **THOM PAIN (BASED ON NOTHING) by Will Eno.** An ordinary man muses on childhood, yearning, disappointment and loss, as he draws the audience into his last-ditch plea for empathy and enlightenment. "It's one of those treasured nights in the theater—treasured nights anywhere, for that matter—that can leave you both breathless with exhilaration and...in a puddle of tears." –*NY Times*. "Eno's words...are familiar, but proffered in a way that is constantly contradictory to our expectations. Beckett is certainly among his literary ancestors." –*nytheatre.com*. [1M] ISBN: 0-8222-2076-8

★ **THE LONG CHRISTMAS RIDE HOME by Paula Vogel.** Past, present and future collide on a snowy Christmas Eve for a troubled family of five. "...[a] lovely and hauntingly original family drama...a work that breathes so much life into the theater." –*Time Out*. "...[a] delicate visual feast..." –*NY Times*. "...brutal and lovely...the overall effect is magical." –*NY Newsday*. [3M, 3W] ISBN: 0-8222-2003-2

DRAMATISTS PLAY SERVICE, INC.
440 Park Avenue South, New York, NY 10016 212-683-8960 Fax 212-213-1539
postmaster@dramatists.com www.dramatists.com